# THE CORPORATE DRAMA

Manishdatta Rajul

BlueRose Publishers
NewDelhi • London

First Published in July 2021

ISBN: 978-93-5472-142-7

BLUEROSE PUBLISHERS
www.bluerosepublishers.com
info@bluerosepublishers.com
+91 8882 898 898

Cover Design:
Muskan Sachdeva

Typographic Design:
Ilma Mirza

Distributed by: BlueRose, Amazon, Flipkart

# Dedication

*This book is dedicated to all those young professionals who took their first step into the corporate world and to all those students who can't wait to explore this world.*

# Table of Contents:

# Introduction

One of the significant concerns that the current young professionals face is how to excel in the corporate working environment. The same goes for the students who just can't wait to step into this world, but if we question them if they know what it's going to be out there in the corporate world, they do not have the slightest idea.

This problem arises because, in college studies, the current educational system has ensured that the students gain complete knowledge related to their respective field of interest. But, they forgot to include subjects that can help them be more comfortable and confident in the corporate world.

Whenever I talk to any of my old friends or a buddying junior from my alma mater, I always find most of them struggle and do not have good clarity on what's going on in their professional life. Mostly, they are just trying to go with the flow, wherever the company management pushes their career, which might be beneficial to the company, but that may not be true from the individual's point of view. With such an approach, you lose your choice because it is not you who made the call on what happens with your career growth.

You cannot pinpoint a single person and blame them for such a working culture in the corporate because it will not solve the problem, and now, the time for the same has been already passed. Such practices have been going long before any one of us cared about the process. This has happened with our parents, and the same with their parents as well. It might be the reason that our parents usually have a piece of advice for every single action that we take. But our parents gave no advice to us in regards to how to become successful in a corporate working environment.

It is not that people lack the skills required or the knowledge to perform their jobs properly. The majority of the people having a corporate job are capable of fulfilling their job responsibilities appropriately. Also, they have the most genuine intentions to do their job and not to be a laggard. But they lack the skills to showcase their final work and display their true potential in front of the top management. They miss out on small opportunities, which could bring them in highlights and have successful career progression within the corporate world. They miss out on opportunities to climb the corporate ladder. They also sometimes become victims of office politics or do not get a manager who pushes them in the right direction towards a successful career. So many times, people can accomplish big but do not have the experience to adjust to the corporate culture and thrive in this ruthless environment.

Every few weeks or so, I come across a friend, colleague or a relative struggling in the corporate world and has now denounced it as a hellish experience. I will console them, hear their plea and would suggest some small changes that can benefit them in performing well in their corporate job. It is not like that they cannot complete a task correctly. They are already good or at least okay in the corporate world, but these small changes help them showcase their positive side and be better employees.

But if everyone is struggling in a way or so in the corporate work environment, then there is definitely a need for something, which can guide these young professionals in their corporate journey. During this period, I came across a TEDx video given by Chandler bolt, CEO of Self-Publishing School, where he showcases that a single book brings changes to the lives of at least 1200 people. And then I found my solution. I decided to write a book that could help people bridge the knowledge gap through tried and tested methods, which provides them simple yet sophisticated steps to be a star performer in their corporate job. Please think of this book as a guidebook, as we have for tourist places, which provides tips and suggestions to have a wonderful experience and make it a pleasant journey. In the same way, the purpose of this book would be to guide through small nuances of the corporate world.

So here we are. In this book, I will cover the different vital aspects of corporate life in three sections. These sections will answer your questions about

1. How to improve yourself?
2. How to improve your relationship with other stakeholders such as your manager, colleagues, etc.? and

3. How to have a peaceful work life?

I have written this book by taking notes from my experiences in the corporate world and taking notes from other more experienced people in this domain. This is done to ensure we have taken into account the complete spectrum of the corporate culture.

But before we proceed any further, I have an important disclaimer to make. This book is written based on the experiences that I have gained as a practising manager. I have tried to cover the experiences of other senior leaders and experiences shared with me by my friends and colleagues. Thus, I would request you to assess the situation before implementing any recommendations mentioned in this book. The suggestions given in this book are not scientifically validated on a larger audience, and it is mainly, what I believe in. If you do not correlate with me, you can follow the path that suits you better because the contents of this book are based on the experiences that I have gained from corporate life.

If you do like this book, then consider this book as a stepping stone for your corporate life. It will make the corporate journey – less hellish and more enjoyable. The purpose of this book is to provide methods to the reader to be more professional and presentable.

# Building a Profile

Most working professionals consider a regular job meaningless and boring. It is believed that your job should always be linked to a passion to make it interesting. It is not your fault in thinking that a career with passion is the only way to have an ideal job. The entertainment media has emphasised this concept of having a career with a passion so much that they made routine jobs look like a pathetic way of living.

But the fact is that the job feels boring if you make it all about work or the level of service that you are providing to the company. This approach can make anything worthless.

Consider you are playing football, you are good at it, and it brings joy to you. You forget all your worries when you are playing a game of football. When you are trying to make a goal, it feels like this is it. This is what you are meant to be doing your whole life. You feel alive. But if you connect this simple act of playing a sport to work, the feeling will change drastically. Instead of thinking of it as a game, think that you are given a task to push a ball from one end of the field to another, and after half time, again to the opposite end. To make it difficult, you have colleagues who are ready to steal that ball from you so that you cannot achieve your goal quickly and do not get an appraisal from the management. But there are players from your team, just like you have your team members in your office, who can support you and help push the ball faster to the other end, and it's all about the sync between the team members. Now see, suddenly a joyous and adventurous game like football becomes a cumbersome job to do. If everyone pitches the football this way, then in no time, this sport will definitely die.

So always make your job less about work, but more about achieving something. You are a part of an ecosystem at the office. You are working to bring something fruitful to the world and make hundreds of people's lives simpler. The goal of achieving a target always brings the adrenaline rush to anything you do, in the same way, a simple game of pushing a ball but towards a target, towards a goal; becomes the world's most famous game.

A football player needs to have the necessary skills to at least get selected in a team. The player also has to keep learning skills and master them to be in the top playing eleven team players. In the same way, in your corporate jobs, you must possess all the required technical and management skills needed to perform the job satisfactorily. But to be relevant to the firm in the long run, it is also necessary that you keep learning and keep developing new skills that help you finish the job faster and more efficiently.

Learning is essential, but the actual value addition lies in continuous learning and to make yourself updated about the new technological advances in your job profile. This provides you with a cutting edge over all other employees.

Not just learning a skill, but how to apply those to your daily work routine is also important. For example, a simple skill of writing is known to many, but some use this skill to write a book, some use this to write a poem and some to write an editorial. Thus, knowing a skill is important, but applying it in a relevant manner to your job profile is even more critical. The same goes with other skills as well, like many people know how to speak, but some people use it to narrate a story, and others use it to sing a song. Both depend on your interest and what you are trying to achieve.

In a corporate environment, skills can be divided into two types. First, there are role-specific skills that include the technical know-how and the product knowledge of a domain. The definition of these skills may differ as the technology changes, the market evolves, or as the product configuration changes. Thus, you must always remain up to date with the current market trends and the dynamic changes in your field. The second set of skills are managerial skills. You cannot learn this set of skills just by reading or researching about it. This set of skills is more about the experience and situation presented in front of you. Multiple variables may play a role in this, and gaining these skills ensures that you handle the situation professionally. Thus, the best way to gain managerial skills is always by being in the field. The more you face uncomfortable situations, the more you apply these skills, the more you learn, and the more you get better at it. The earlier you become familiar with these situations, the more beneficial it is for you to succeed in corporate life.

The biggest mistake that most people make while learning these skills is that people want to become perfect as soon as they start working on them. They always remain afraid of making any mistakes that might ruin their chances of a promotion or a raise. But by doing so, you do not become familiar with many uncomfortable situations that make you more experienced. The mistakes you make in your early career life always teaches you valuable lessons. In turn, you become more capable of handling such situations when you are at a senior level position in the future.

There is an article in Harvard Business Review which showcases the perfect examples of learning from mistakes.[1] The article not just highlights the importance of learning from mistakes but also the correct way of learning. Many managers think that learning from mistakes is straightforward. You reflect on the mistakes that you have made and note down the points for not repeating the same mistakes again in the future. But the same mistakes do happen by some other teams or in some other project. The reason behind that is we miss out on context-specific learning. Many factors play a role in a project, and all these factors may change in another project; thus, these variances need to be accounted for to

---

[1] "Strategies for Learning from Failure" by Amy C. Edmondson, HBR April 2011 https://hbr.org/2011/04/strategies-for-learning-from-failure

stop repeating the mistakes that lead to failure in the project.

Every child from the start learns that admitting mistakes means taking the complete blame on yourself. This thinking gets ingrained since childhood, and you make decisions keeping this in your mind. Thus, even though you reward employees for learning from mistakes at the corporate level, still, people do not showcase that and do not follow this step. You must ensure that the rewards are fully realised so that learning from mistakes can happen in the true sense, and senior management should appreciate this culture.

This brings us to the next important question: if learning from failure rewards, then should one avoid making mistakes and give their best performance, or should one make mistakes and then rectify them to gain the additional rewards from the company?

The answer lies in identifying the types of mistakes. Not all mistakes would be praiseworthy. Some mistakes will be blameworthy. Failures which happened because an individual chose to violate the defined process are blameworthy. In contrast, failures which occurred because people were trying to explore something new and out of the box are praiseworthy. Suppose mistakes happened because of a lack of clarity. But by making this mistake, people learned something new and will be more cautious in the future to avoid such big mistakes. So this small mistake becomes beneficial for the organisation and is definitely a praiseworthy mistake. The senior management needs to define clear benchmarks for the errors, and then only they will be able to identify which errors are making the organisation grow by learning from failures.

The thing is, you are bound to make mistakes. No one is perfect, and if you are handling something important or of a new domain in a company, then there are even higher chances that you will make some errors, here and there. This will only make you a domain expert because, with the mistakes, the learning part comes naturally. So making a mistake is not always harmful if they are genuine or unavoidable at first. But the important thing is that you learn from these mistakes. Your target should always be to make better mistakes and not to repeat the same ones.

As rightly said by Lily Aldrin in 'How I Met Your Mother' that "There are certain things in life where you know it's a mistake, but you don't really know it's a mistake because the only way to know it's a mistake is to make a mistake and look back and say, "Yep! That was a mistake.""

The same is applicable in your corporate life as well. But the important thing is that your company will be bearing the cost of your mistakes. Thus, it is also crucial that you have all justifications and analysis done to ensure that you reduce your chances of making a mistake, and you should have your concrete reasons for the error that occurred in a project.

If you have studied the Toyota Production System (TPS), then you would know the basis of TPS lies in rectifying the mistake as soon as it occurs. This system stops us from making big regretful mistakes in the future. In a car production, the whole assembly line is stopped to rectify even the smallest mistakes before they get big. The entire system works on detecting failure as early as possible. Even if this leads to a loss of revenue initially, but gradually it makes the system so robust that it brings out zero defect products and ultimate customer satisfaction.

To ensure that you make fewer mistakes, or let's say that you make only genuine mistakes, you must start learning from other people's actions and mistakes. Taking additional courses that help you work on case studies can also improve your decision-making acumen. There are few autobiographies of some of the most outstanding leaders like Steve Jobs, Jeff Bezos, Elon Musk, etc., that you should read. These books will help you understand that everyone has made some mistakes in their career, and some mistakes were more significant than others, but what matters is what you do after that. Did you repeat the same mistakes, or you took lessons from them and became much wiser?

To aid the process of learning faster and make fewer mistakes, you can even join few online courses related to your domain. The sites like Coursera, LinkedIn Learning and online Certification sites can help you significantly in finding the relevant courses. Many organisations even have internal classes that are structured according to their internal working culture. They also tie-up with online learning websites to ensure that the employees gain skill at ease.

You can never complete the task of building a good profile in a single day. You have to make continuous efforts in learning all the required job-specific knowledge and managerial skills as well. These skills will help you in delivering better results consistently with much ease.

# The Three Basic Skills

In our regular lives, to sustain, we need three essential elements, i.e., Food, Water and Air. In the same way, to be efficient in corporate life, we need three essential management skills, which are

1. Time Management,
2. Ability to put across your point, and
3. Presentation skills

The way we can have alternatives to food, water and air. Similarly, these management skills are not mandatory, but knowing how to use these three skills will make your life way more accessible in excelling in the job assigned to you. These skills will help you plan better, communicate better, and systematically showcase your work to achieve the desired career growth.

The skills related to your job profile are important, but these three basic skills will form the basis for that, and no matter what you do in your job or what profile you choose to be in, these skills will always be there at your perusal to make your corporate life a lot smoother.

The students who are pursuing management degrees from the Tier-1 business schools already have some knowledge about this. But anyone can learn these skills because the importance is not knowing what these are. But the importance lies in knowing how to use them in a stable job environment. Embedding these skills into your work life can only happen through experience.

So what's so important about these skills? We will see that in detail in the following few pages to understand these skills.

## Time Management

Everyone has the same amount of time in a day and would like to dedicate only a fixed amount of time to the work, as we have to make sure that we fulfil our personal lives' responsibilities as well. Thus, in this context, Time Management becomes prioritising the limited amount of time available to us to accomplish the maximum amount of work with the highest priority assigned as part of our job profile. In short, to achieve more in less amount of time.

I realised the importance of Time Management when I was pursuing my MBA degree from IIM Bangalore. Start from day one, we had so many things to cater to that it felt like we are living a life of a week in a single day. We juggled academics, extra-curricular, club events, assignments, project works, and parties; all at once. In reality, academics was never a burden. But dealing with the rest of the things gave us a nightmare.

In the first two semesters, things were incredibly tight scheduled that we didn't think that we have time even to take a breath. So students come up with bizarre ideas to get additional times in their daily schedule. Some students would start skipping breakfasts or dinners to get that extra ten minutes to complete some pending work. Other students have their own way of sacrificing something else to make for the lost time. This is where the actual management learning we gain and time management played a significant role in thriving in that environment.

It took time to accept that we are not superhuman, and everyone has limitations. The only solution to complete tasks is to prioritise the tasks as per the time available. The secret to being successful in such scenarios is not by completing all the tasks but by ensuring that you finish the most critical tasks concerning your short term or long-term goals. Therefore, just by prioritising the daily schedules and with some time to get used to this activity makes everyone comfortable in the management studies environment.

Students usually get comfortable from the third term when their Summer Internship Placements are over. There is a bit less pressure from additional activities that we used to do in the first two terms. So students think that they are at peace because they have fewer things to do. But in reality, they underestimate their calibre, and they do not realise that now they have mastered the art of time management. They realise their true potential when just after the summer internship, they come back to college to continue their second year of management studies. Now the things are the same; the activities to be done are the same, everyone has to look after academics, club events, extra-curricular participation, and so on. But they still manage to do all of this and with a lot of ease. This is when we realise the importance of learning how to manage time, and it's not just a skill but an art.

The most important thing about time management is that it is not rocket science, and anyone can learn this. All you have to do is implement few fundamental rules into your regular daily activities. Eventually, as time will pass, this skill will become one of the most crucial parts of your successes. It will be helpful throughout your life, no matter what job domain you are in and whether it is for personal or professional requirements.

## The three fundamental rules for time management:

1. Small tasks which take less than 2 minutes must be finished as soon as they come.
2. The Pareto Principle must be applied everywhere. Always prioritise and complete activities that take less than twenty percent of your time but completes more than 80 percent of your work. Once these tasks are finished, then and then only you should work on the less important tasks.
3. As you get comfortable in your job profile, start taking more tasks or asking your manager to allocate you a more extensive profile. The benefit of bringing more tasks in your bucket is that you get the opportunity to master the skill of Time Management

through practice and build your profile simultaneously. So always be on a lookout to take on more responsibilities within the team to help you grow your career.

## Put your point across the table

You can see that all CXO level people possess one extremely important skill: communicating their views/opinions in a crystal clear manner. As a matter of fact, these people are at CXO level positions because of this skill only, which played a significant role in their career progression.

There are two key aspects to this skill. First, having clarity on your thoughts and ensuring other people understand your point of view, and second, having that courage to put your point in front of everyone during the discussion.

Some people have this skill from the start, while some acquire this after few years working in the corporate environment, but everyone masters this skill only by experience. Being confident and having clarity of thoughts are the only two things required to put your point during the meeting, group discussion, or in a heated conversation.

Many times, people say that their boss cannot understand or his manager is unreasonable, but that happens with all the people. Your manager has multiple tasks at hand, and he does not have time to pay more than 30 seconds of his attention to understand your problem. Thus, in such situations, it becomes highly crucial to express your opinion in a precise manner. Every word that you speak or write should be thought of clearly beforehand. Remember, your manager will always consider you of lesser intelligence if you can't understand his asks on the first go. Also, he will consider you only of lesser intelligence if you cannot make him understand your point in the first instance itself. You should always gain knowledge for any particular subject/problem to such a level that you can make a five-year-old child understand the concept. If you possess the understanding to such a level, then you definitely have mastered the subject, and no one will counter that.

The only way to master this skill of putting your point across the table is with experience, and the more you practice, the less time it will eventually take yours to draft a sentence. The importance of this skill increases drastically the more your climb the corporate ladder. It becomes challenging to convey your point to a person who is at CXO level because he has even lesser time. On the other hand, when you get to the CXO level, it becomes even more crucial to put your thoughts in a short and simple to understand manner. This enables you to ensure that your employees are in sync with you, and you can save the company's time by not repeating the same things again and again.

## Presentation Skills

The presentation skills mean how you use software to present your idea in a more elaborative manner. The presentation skills help convey the concept precisely the way you want and remove the uncertainties in understanding your idea. For example, if you ask your audience to imagine a beach, then everyone will think of a beach in their mind, but the exact scenery might differ. Some will think of the locations they have visited during their trips, while others might think of something they dream about or what they think a beach would look like in reality. Thus, it becomes important how you present an idea of a beach, so that audience can relate to your story that you will communicate related to that specific beach.

You can present your idea using any of the currently available software in the market. It can be a presentation/slides consisting of text and images, or it can simply be a text-heavy word document that thoroughly elaborates every detail in the form of sentences, or it can be an excel that is full of numbers.

The choice of medium/software depends on your requirement and what suits your idea. All these software are equally important. Depending on the need, one or the other will always come in handy.

When you think of an example of the best leaders who can put their ideas in front of an audience in the best way possible, Steve Jobs will definitely top that list. The elegance he possessed when he was on the stage is just unmatchable. Many have tried to achieve that feat, even Elon Musk has tried the same things, but it is undeniable that Steve Jobs has his own charisma that brought every idea and concept together in a fluent and lucid manner. Every word that he spoke showcased the confidence that he has in his products, and the way he introduced the new additions to the Apple product family is just extraordinary. I would recommend that you should watch the way he introduced the world with iPhone and Macbook Laptops. It was just magnificent.

To master the art of presenting an idea/thoughts, currently, there are multiple learning courses available in the market via Coursera, LinkedIn Learning and courses provided by your company. As part of the employee learning program, many companies have self-curated courses which suit to their company's requirement. You can even resort to YouTube videos as well, as they can give you ample ideas. But you can become better at using this software, only when you start using them on a regular basis and then you will learn the Nitty-gritty of these softwares.

The three basic skills discussed in this chapter will pave the path to make a better impression in your professional career. These skills always come in handy to complete a task in a better way and also to reduce the amount of time it requires to deliver this task. These skills bring discipline in your approach to tackle a work, which brings peace, as the level of certainty reduces significantly.

It takes years of experience and systematic efforts to become good at what you do. In this process, the sense of achievement plays a major which is almost in all cases becomes the underlying driving force in achieving a better career path.

# Sense of Achievement

Almost all professionals are intelligent and hard-working, or at least they have the capability to perform the task properly for the job profile they have been hired for. They all have gone through multiple screening processes, which include online as well as offline process. After going through numerous rounds of the interview process of online assessment, offline tests, group discussion, and personal interview, then only a candidate gets selected for a job. So, if a candidate has shown his mettle through all these processes, then why does it happen that the same candidate cannot always give his/her 100% at the corporate job.

It's not that they have cheated in the examination. At least not every one of them can cheat. But still, many fail at their corporate job. Most of the professionals complain that they are not happy. Also, they have proved their mettle through the screening processes, so they are intelligent and hard-working, and that's established. So, what is forbidding them to put the same level of effort into the corporate job? What stops them from performing well and being a star-performer?

The single factor missing in the recipe of being a star performer is the motivation or willingness to perform well. Many times, the corporate environment misses out on giving a sense of achievement to their employees. They provide a good package, better perks and the best working space in the office. But they miss out on acknowledging their employees, which in turn does not provide a sense of achievement to their employees.

If you find a good candidate for a company, and if they have always performed well in their academic and professional life, then hardly will it be a case that the candidate has been motivated by only the monetary perks. But getting recognised in the organisation for the hard work they have put in also plays a significant role.

The thing is, getting a sense of achievement is imbibed in almost everything where progress matters. From childhood only, the children get accustomed to such an environment where appreciation matters. Children spend most of their early years playing a game. For example, take any game, let's take Mario Video Game[2], in which every player knows that the purpose of the game is to save the princess. But the developers didn't make the game so that it happens in a single sitting. They have given multiple chapters and at least three levels within each chapter. You get points and extra lives after you cross each level or if you do something extra in a game like finding the easter eggs. These rewards make the game easy and super-fun. Suddenly the game is not about saving the princess, but it's more about clearing the levels present at hand, one at a time.

---

[2] "Super Mario Bros" – Electronic game created by Nintendo Company Ltd.
https://www.britannica.com/topic/Super-Mario-Bros

Having multiple levels or checkpoints in a job provides a direction on how to accomplish the same. You can find similar arrangements in your school, in your college or mainly in any large structured working environment. You do not finish school in 12 years. Just think, if someone advertises that enrol your kid for a 12-year schooling program, then it will be hard even to visualise what will happen in 12 years. But instead, people just take one year at a time for a challenge, and the kid focuses on the tasks that are aligned in the next year ahead. To bring further clarity and simplicity to the course, the kid concentrates only on the next three months because each standard has multiple terms and examinations. You can see for yourself that even a simple schooling structure has multiple standards of education and numerous exams in it; and a complete structure to it. The same structure that we had in the Mario video game. I am not saying that one is copying this from another, but almost all large assignments or programs need this structure of dividing a bigger task into smaller assignments to accomplish the end goal of finishing it.

Even in college, the same structure is followed so that students have clearly defined goals ahead of them. This way, it is easier for the students to focus on the target ahead, and it also provides a clear update on their progress. You can even change your direction or decide in between with the feedback you receive through multiple examinations, whether you need to study even harder to score better or change your discipline, which aligns with your interests.

The same thing applies to our job as well. Getting smaller tasks so that you do not get overwhelmed and clearing those small-small tasks results in more significant results. This makes the final job at hand a bit simpler and more enjoyable. In addition to this, you always feel motivated to perform these smaller tasks because the checkered flag is always visible to you and the end goal feels achievable. But the actual problem is that not many corporates align their goal to such smaller tasks, then; how do you deal with such situations?

There are so many employees in an organisation, and for a team to focus on assigning smaller tasks to each individual is just impossible to do. Then, how come a school curriculum is prepared with specific small tasks for lakhs of students? The difference here is that a school curriculum more or less remains the same for each year. Thus, it is commercially feasible to create a curriculum once, which will be implemented for years to come and will remain more or less the same. But in corporate organisations, every employee, or at least not more than a group, has a different set of goals and that too for each year. Also, the yearlong goals assigned to an employee may change at any time as the organisation's priorities change or as per the changing market dynamics. So, this leaves us limited options to make our priorities clear.

To make things simpler and to have clearly defined timelines, you can always divide your tasks by yourself. You can check and see the major deliverables in an assigned job, and then you make that job divided into these deliverables. You focus on achieving these one or two deliverable at a time, and slowly and steadily, you complete the whole job. The benefit of this approach is that you can apply this to any job.

The most important benefit of this approach is that it gives you a breathing period. You divide your task into smaller ones with a timeline to achieve them. Your timeline to accomplish these smaller tasks should coincide with your final goal and deadline, so that you achieve your end goal within the deadline assigned. Now, whenever you finish your smaller tasks within your timelines, you get a breathing period to take a short break or relax. You know that you are as per the schedule, and you will deliver the final result. Thus, a short break to recharge yourself is viable and is one of the most required privileges to be effective at all time.

The second benefit is that you never hit panic mode. You know you have clear defined small achievable tasks in front of you. You also have a clearly defined timeline to achieve all these small tasks to complete your final bigger task. Thus, you just have to focus on finishing these small tasks within the timeline, and everything will be fine then. If you miss a timeline of any small tasks, then you can buckle up, cover your time in the following small tasks and then get a breathing period.

This minuscule activity of dividing your tasks into smaller ones and creating a timeline might feel cumbersome at the start, but the benefits outweigh it drastically. At the beginning of every project, implementing this simple method will bring you into the comfort zone in any job assigned to you. A sample check sheet is mentioned below for your reference. You can prepare a similar sheet for your ongoing tasks by making the required changes in the below sample.

| S. No. | Task Description | Expected Deal Value | Final Deal Value | Checkpoint 1 | Checkpoint 2 | Checkpoint 3 | Checkpoint 4 | Checkpoint 5 | Checkpoint 6 |
|---|---|---|---|---|---|---|---|---|---|
| 1 | Task 1 | X | X | Done | Done | Done | Pending | Not Required | Pending |
| 2 | Task 2 | X | X | Done | Done | Pending | Not Required | Pending | Pending |
| 3 | Task 3 | X | X | Done | Done | Not Required | Done | Done | Pending |
| 4 | Task 4 | X | X | Done | Done | Done | Done | Pending | Pending |
| 5 | Task 5 | X | X | Finished | | | | | |

*i: Sample Check Sheet for tasks*

The sheet mentioned above also helps in keeping track of the completed tasks which you might require during the appraisal time.

The work-life is way longer than our school or college life. It is actually double the total combined time that we spent studying. Thus, it becomes even more important to be motivated at all times, and a sense of achievement plays a significant role in it. Therefore, the goals must be divided and accordingly assigned so that you are always in control of your corporate work-life.

In the corporate environment, there always going to be something or another which will test your capabilities. It may be your boss or the job assigned to you, or someone outside your organisation. But do not get demotivated at such times, and it becomes even more critical to remain focus on what you do. Always be passionate to prove your mettle, to be at the top of your game and never back down from anything. Always be ready to crack a deal, achieve the impossible and be a superhero. Nothing gets you more pumped-up than to successfully clear a task that everyone thought cannot be done. Such jobs give an extra boost to your career growth. This approach will differentiate you from the rest of the pack. In any case, if you were not able to finish it, then still it is important that you tried and you learned something new from it. Thomas Edison took more than 2000 attempts to create the first successful bulb using a carbon filament instead of a carbon rod, and in the end, he didn't think that he failed 2000 times, but now he knew 2000 ways from which a bulb can't be created. That's the kind of thinking you have to employ in your working environment. Because whether you have finished a task successfully or not, you will definitely learn something from it that will help you grow in corporate life.

But what if you do not find such opportunities, then what to do? We will cover this topic in-depth in the next chapter on how to bring the best out of yourself and get things done? How to find opportunities which aid you in the process of becoming the best?

## Getting things done

Everyone wants to bring their best and get that employee of the month/quarter/year acknowledgement in their career. But the only struggle they face is that they do not have time to complete that job to make them stand out. The real problem is that we are doing a lot and we are justifying the salary that the company is paying with the current tasks in hand. We usually measure our productivity with the time spent doing office chores, and we forget that real productivity is measured with the outcome or the results delivered. A factory's productivity is measured not by how many hours the machines are working but by measuring the amount of final product produced from the factory that is saleable.

Similarly, it would help if you also focused on the result you are delivering to the company, whether in terms of the additional sales you are bringing to the company or closing some new initiatives to bring cost savings. These things define how valuable an asset you are to the company and not by the time you spend for the company. Because when we measure productivity with respect to time, then the people who are spending more time to finish the same job will come out as more productive as they are dedicating more of their time to the company. Now even you know that this is an absurdly false way of measuring productivity.

You are doing a valuable work or not, can be measured by checking whether your career or job assigned to you, ensures that the company achieves their annual targets. If the company's target is to cut their cost so that they can utilise this money to increase the product portfolio, and if as a manager you are working on initiatives that will ensure that money will not be used on waste products, then you are aligned with your company's primary goal, and you are doing a valuable job. But if the company's focus is on being compliant with the policies enforced by the auditors and the government. This may include the trivial task of uploading all contracts into the central depository. But instead of working on that. You are working on bringing cost efficiencies by skipping operational processes. Then definitely, your work is tarnishing the company's goal rather than benefitting it. Being compliant may win the Board of Directors' trust, but if you are skipping the operation process to close the deal, then this is not a valuable use of time.

This answers our question in the last chapter: what to do if we do not find opportunities to progress in the career or do meaningful work in the organisation?

The answer is simple. You have to take responsibility for yourself. If an organisation is not focusing on you, then you have to take matters into your hand. The first thing you could do is take additional responsibilities that ensure you get meaningful work to do that is aligned with your organisation's goals. You think you do not have time, but believe me, you do, and I speak by learning from my and several other professional's careers. The thing is until you get additional work, till then you keep working inefficiently. So, when the work increases, you start bringing productivity. You automate few tasks. You align certain things. You begin streamlining the few older processes so that the uncertainty reduces. These steps help you in focusing on newer assigned tasks. If your luck favours and the extra responsibility assigned is significantly big, then you might get one or two direct subordinates to help you out on the job. Now, just look at yourself. You are now working on key initiatives related to process reengineering, and you are also handling additional responsibilities. No company will dare to ignore such good work from an employee.

If you see the relationship between Steve Jobs and Tim Cooks at a big company like Apple Inc., you will find a similar example. Steve Jobs had a very high standard for all of his requirements, and it was none less than a superhero task to achieve his accolades. But within the same organisation, Tim Cook consistently delivered exceptional results to bring higher productivity. He was always ready to take on the more crucial tasks, and his works made his name within the organisation. Eventually, his dedication and consistent performance paid off, and Tim Cook took over the reign as the CEO of Apple Inc. from Steve Jobs in 2011. This is one of the best examples where even though Tim had a very rigid and stringent leader, he still managed to gain corporate growth through persistence and by taking more daunting tasks than the last ones in his career.

To bring productivity, you just have to keep in mind that you will be spending 45 hours a week or nine days hours a day at the corporate job. So, just spend that time doing something productive and not by taking multiple breaks in the cafeteria. It is as simple as that.

If you are still not finding something meaningful to do by taking additional responsibilities, if your tasks are only increasing and you are not feeling motivated, then it is better to switch the role or the team. If required, then change the company altogether in search of a better role.

Life is so small and for the rest of your life, if you're spending one-third of your life in the corporate environment, then let's make it worthwhile.

A few years back, one of my friends had the same feeling. He completed his engineering from the civil engineering branch, but he was nowhere motivated to explore career opportunities in this field. Even when he was pursuing an engineering degree, he was more interested in mechanical engineering than civil. But he did not score good marks in the entrance exam, so he has to settle with the civil branch instead of getting mechanical. I guess this is why he did not score well in engineering because he was not motivated enough to study hard in this field. So, during campus placements, he did not opt for any company offering a job in the civil engineering field. Instead, he took a job in a sales profile.

While working as a sales executive, he realised that this work is not value-adding to his desired career growth. This profile will not enable him to deliver the best he could because he was not motivated enough. So, he looked for opportunities related to the mechanical branch, like in the supply chain division, to finally settle in the field of his choice. Eventually, he got a job in a start-up to manage the demand-supply planning and look after the vendor development field. As the role was of his choice so without wasting a single day, he made the switch. He took the risk of switching to a start-up that was only six months old. But he worked hard every day and delivered the best results that he could, which all senior management people appreciated. After six years of graduating, he settled finally in a big company with a good salary package. But most importantly, he is now settled in the field of his choice, where he is enjoying every single day working for the company.

The single most crucial decision he took was to take control of his life and explore opportunities that suited him. He might have settled in the civil engineering field during the campus placements. But that would not have been fair to him as well as to the company, as the performance will not be up to mark because his interest was somewhere else.

Getting a job in a field of your interest automatically motivates you to deliver the best job that you can. You work not for the money but to prove your mettle. This approach also helps in building a good rapport within the team. But still, sometimes people face issue in making a good impression within the company. The problem lies not in the level of effort you put in but in how you approach a problem.

The best way to create a positive image within your team is by changing your approach from a problem-oriented to a solution-oriented employee. No one wants to spend time with a guy who brings the problem to them, but everyone loves the guy who brings the solution along with the problem to them. Thus, before presenting a problem that you are facing, always think through it to arise at a solution. If not the solution, then try to create at least three possible actions to solve the problem. This approach helps in creating your own understanding about the issue. If you have noticed, this approach will also touch upon the topic discussed in the previous chapter, i.e. sense of achievement. If some solution is getting implemented to get rid of a problem, then this approach will be your solution, or at least you have taken part in the discussion and made it easier for the team to arrive at the solution. Thus, you are getting involved in the decision-making process, and you are not some random employee to do the grunt work. Always make your brain work, and that's the only way to grow and get experienced. Because by thinking through a situation, you get accustomed to the problems where you know both, the solution that works and the options that might fail.

In the corporate environment, nothing can beat hard work, but smart work will help you to take on newer tasks and extra responsibility. We are living in the 21st century, and if you can think of something, then definitely it is doable. I mean that if you can get the details ready and plan of execution, nothing can stop you from achieving it. Thus, in your work profile, always try to automate non-value adding and repetitive tasks. Like I handle the sourcing portfolio, so for the repetitive buying requirements, I always create a rate card with the partner so that the user team can raise purchase requisition, and purchase order can be issued to the partner automatically within the defined turnaround time. All negotiations happen at once to bring entire cost savings in one go and are required to be validated by the finance team one time only. Thus, crucial time saved for everyone. If you cannot relate to this example, then do not worry. What I was trying to say is that you can always find ways to reduce your grunt work so that you can focus on tasks where you apply your brain and create value for yourself and the company.

Smart work is more or less related to the time management skill that we talked about in the previous chapters. You have to prioritise the tasks that are important to you and then automate the redundant or repetitive tasks, especially those tasks that are less important. These bottoms of the list tasks need to be performed; otherwise, you get escalations, but completing them on time does not add much value to your domain.

Thus, it is always better to find an alternative yet better solution so that your manual work gets reduced and time gets freed up to take additional responsibilities.

For the remaining important tasks, keep a tab on the deadlines and always complete them on time. Because you must never lose focus on proving your mettle and get rewarded. Sometimes very minute mistakes may ruin your whole work, and you do not get credit for that. Thus, you mustn't leave any loose ends. Think of it this way, that engineers who are working on the space shuttle do not have any margin to make an error because people's life is at stake. Same way, take your job seriously and deliver the tasks assigned to you with utmost perfection.

It is important to know that to get things done, everything boils downs to one and one only thing, and this is being effective. Thus, it is more important to know how to be effective, and we will discuss this in the next chapter.

# Being Effective

Being effective is nothing but how you utilise your time effectively or in the best possible way you can. One of the easiest yet most effective ways to do that is to apply Pareto Principle in your life. You might have heard this in the name of the 80-20 rule, where you achieve 80% of the results by spending 20% of your time or resources available. The best thing about this principle is that it applies to anything you do, and I mean anything literally.

For example, in a company, 80% of work is performed by 20% of employees. The cost of the top 20% of material in a factory constitutes 80% of the cost. The time taken to complete 80% of the work usually takes 20% of your total time, but to make it perfect and to achieve 100%, you have to dedicate the rest of 80% of your time as well. Just to be clear on this principle, if you have spent 10 hours completing a task, then if the accuracy required in that task is 80% only, then you might have finished the same task in 2 hours only. The additional 8 hours were required to double or triple check the work for error and to make the work presentable.

Let's take another example, along with a chart diagram to give you a better understanding. I have taken this example from asq.org.

In the above diagram, data were collected regarding the customer complaints received for the five categories. You can easily see that the maximum complaint was received in the Documents and Product Quality category, which amounts to approximately eighty percent of the total complaints received. So to effectively resolve the most complaints in the shortest amount of time, the company has to work on these two categories first. Now, there may be multiple subcategories within these categories as well. The below diagram provides the details about the sub-categories within the Documents category.

Within the Documents category, you can see that eighty percent of customer complaints are only for two types of error, i.e. Quality Certificate Error and Quality Certificate Missing. Thus, the Pareto principle helped the company in this case to identify the complaints which can be resolved in the least amount of time to achieve maximum customer satisfaction. The remaining errors also need to be rectified to make the process hundred percent error-free. But with this principle, we were able to identify the most recurring complaints and by prioritising the resolution of these complaints helped the company to address maximum customer complaints and to avoid the same in the future.

This principle is very standard and usually applied at all levels. Like I handle the sourcing portfolio, where we attend the cost savings initiative for top 20% items to bring 80% of the savings and topmost initiatives are addressed first so that our time is spent in the most effective way. After completing all these tasks, then we move forward to the rest of the low-end initiatives as time permits.

You can apply the same principle to achieve your targets at the workplace as well. If there were five tasks and each task requires 10 hours to complete, but you only have 10 hours in total. Then by applying the 80-20 rule, you ensure that you finish 80% of all tasks and achieve the max you can. This is considering that your job does not require you to complete just one but a perfect task. For example, if you are a space engineer in an Aeronautical organisation, then achieving 80% is unacceptable as people's lives are at stake. Anything less than 100% is just not acceptable in such cases.

But if your job is all about allocating the limited time to achieve the best you can, then Pareto Principle is the available option. If we compare the job profiles in any domain for the past 30 years, you can see that fewer people are currently employed to do more jobs because every company wants to be profitable. That is perfectly fine from the organisation point of view. Interestingly, even the organisation accepts that you can't finish all the jobs to the 100% level. But they expect that you devote your time to the most critical activities and bring the best results for the organisation.

But being effective is not just about devoting your time properly but also delivering the results in the stipulated timelines. Deadlines are sacrosanct. Thus, it is important to just focus on the task at hand and deliver it within the deadline.

You might have faced this that many times, you prepare a proper schedule for the tasks that you need to finish in a day. But in the end, you end up doing completely different things. Because in today's workplace, priorities frequently change as per the business requirement. Also, tasks are cross-functional. To deliver an order, multiple teams are working in sync with each other. So when the teams' involvement is high, the dependency on them is also higher. This increases the uncertainty significantly on the activities that you will perform in a day and timelines associated with each of those. Now, because of this, you end up doing completely different work from what you have planned.

An efficient method to work with changing priorities is that you address the most urgent queries only. Tasks that are priorities by the senior management needs to be finished first by you. If there was an ample amount of time, then you could have completed it all without fail. But that was not the case, so we have to prioritise what management wants. People from other teams are working to fulfil their KRAs, and they will prioritise tasks that benefit them. This sometimes results in escalations for tasks that could have been finished in a day or two but were forcibly finished within an hour. Also, this might not result in any value addition in your KRAs. Thus, you have to prioritise the tasks which are required by the senior management and which helps you to achieve higher ratings.

Sometimes, you are not in a good mood to focus on the task at hand and bring it to a finish. It might just be a minuscule task requiring you just to send a simple follow-up mail, but you still resist making that effort because you are just not feeling to put any effort into the tasks. This usually happens when there is no concrete deadline for a task. Like you have to finish it soon, but how soon? This no one has defined for you.

In such cases, create a deadline for yourself. Just give a commitment to the recipient of the requirement, that you will finish this task by so and so date. This fires up your brain to complete the task within the timeline defined by you. You put in your extra effort just so that you meet your commitment, otherwise unlike the rest of the time, this time, the other person is going to chase you because you have given a firm deadline.

If you have heard about Parkinson's Law, then you would know that the amount of work will stretch itself as per the deadline. It means that things will find their way into your schedule as per the deadline. If you have a week to finish a task and the downside of not finishing it is that you might lose your job, then the efforts put by you will be accordingly only. That extra level of commitment will be there from your end to finish that job within a week because a lot is at stake. Now, if for the same work, if a month is given, then you would complete the same work in a month's time only. And that's just nothing but Parkinson's Law. Therefore, you should have a tight deadline, and if nothing is given to you, then assess the task and give a genuine deadline by yourself to the relevant stakeholders.

By setting up a deadline, you get benefits threefold. First, you complete a task within defined timelines, which helps you gain respect within the organisation. Going forward, people will believe what you say, and there won't be unnecessary follow-ups over mail or escalations. Thus, lesser junk mails. Second, one task finished is one task less. Your time will get freed up for other activities as well. So, you will be able to devote more time to the remaining activities, and you can finish them with better results. Thus, less work-related headache and more job clarity. Third, as we have discussed in the previous chapters, you will get a sense of achievement. Your job will be fulfilling. At the end of the day, when you go home, nothing is better than having that feeling that the day was productive. One task that needs to be finished is checked off from the list.

Sometimes to get a job finished within the defined timeline, you might have to check with your subordinates or with employees of other teams. In such cases, you will be surprised by just how much work a follow-up can do. Never underestimate the power of a follow-up. A timely and well-structured follow-up can work significantly in your favour. Also, as you grow within the organisation, a lot depends on how you make your subordinates productive. In such cases, just a simple mail follow-up can enable you to get the task completed by your team. A follow-up should ideally provide ample time to the other person to work on the task, but also, the follow-up should be such that the other person does not forget about the job and takes the assignment on priority. This might depend on the level of the job and job performer. One thing to be cleared on this is that a follow-up mail is entirely different from an escalation mail. A follow-up mail ensures that the other person understands the urgency of the requirement and finishes it on time.

Till now, in this chapter, we have discussed the ways you can become effective. But being effective in the true sense requires that your subordinates become effective as well. They will be doing most of the groundwork, and the more efficient they are, the better results you will be able to deliver as a team.

You bring the best results from your subordinates and think of them as a computer that performs the task as per the commands you have given to them. The better the code you write, the faster and better results will be. Similarly, the more structured instructions you provide to them, the easier it is for them to perform the tasks and deliver an output. Thus, you always ensure that the thinking part needs to be performed by you, and your subordinates can perform the execution. This also ensures that you understand the complete process and do not place unnecessary expectations on them. Also, this works the other way round as well. If you know the entire process, then your subordinates will not be able to fool you around with random excuses. If your associates are working for the designated time on the given job, then this will in itself bring half of the effectiveness. The rest of it depends on how you design the process to perform the task.

By applying this approach, suddenly, the whole perspective changes. Now, you are not just transferring your job to your subordinates, but you are directly involved in it by yourself, and in a sense, you are taking their help because you can't do everything on your own. Your subordinates won't be feeling that they are doing some random job, which half of them do not care or don't know how to do. But actually, they are part of an enormous task, in which everyone is working as a team to deliver the best result together. This approach helps you to earn respect from your team. This also helps in urgent situations to demand more output from your team.

Just remember, whatever things you hate from your boss, just do not transfer those things to your team. And the things you want your boss should do, just do it yourself for your team. This will help you to understand what challenges your boss is facing. Also, by being the best of all, you are making the corporate environment desirable and peaceful. One team at a time, we can make the corporate environment where everyone is happy because the biggest deterrent to being effective is not knowing what to do and how to do it.

The role of a superior that we discussed in the above paragraphs may differ as you move up the corporate ladder. As you start handling more and more responsibility, the less you will be able to get involved in specific jobs. The job becomes more about people management. In such a situation, as always, prioritisation comes to our rescue. You get yourself involved in the most high quality and high-value tasks, and you let your direct reportees handle the rest. But in the meanwhile, it is vital to ensure that you transfer the knowledge of how to manage a team as we discussed in the previous chapters to your direct reportees. And this continues as you grow. Eventually, as the team gets bigger, it also gets better because you have ensured that the whole team is working on a single philosophy of bringing effectiveness.

At senior-level positions, it becomes even more essential to bring effectiveness to the team than just to yourself. The parameters that we have discussed will undoubtedly help you achieve the same systematically.

At a senior level, it is important to bring productivity to the company. To do that, it sometimes may require you to take help from other teams. So be it. Just take help and get the job done. But here one thing you have to notice, that other employees will only go out of their way to support you only if you have done the same thing in the past so that you can achieve your goals, which may or may not coincide with their KRAs. If you had provided help when they needed it in the past, then the chances are that they will support you even higher this time. One cannot be more wrong in underestimating the power of having good and healthy relations within the organisation. You have to consistently perform your level best and try not to depend on others, but you can never be so sure when things may go out of your hands, and you might need some extra help to save the sinking ship or make the job perfect.

So, remember to give help and take help whenever it is required.

Having good relationships with your manager, other employees and colleagues, need a lot more focus and discussion to understand it properly. The things we have discussed in short in the previous paragraph do not justify this topic's importance. Thus, we will discuss this topic in details in the next section.

## Working with a Manager

A manager or a reporting manager is the employee in the company directly in charge of your career growth, learning and goal setting. Thus, it becomes even more important that a particular emphasis needs to be paid into maintaining a good relationship with your manager out of all employees.

A manager can be of two types, i.e., a leader or a boss. You might have read multiple articles mentioning the difference between a leader and a boss on the internet, and believe me, in the corporate environment, all those things will make sense to you. One of the significant difference between a leader and a boss is that a leader has gained that senior-level position by going through a rigorous corporate journey and is always ready to bring changes in the system, which is good for the subordinates. A leader will focus on his/her reportees' career growth and will not take this thing lightly. In Short, a leader is simple to handle because you just have to work smart and hard to bring the best result you can.

But on the other hand, a boss is difficult to manage, and you always have to tread lightly. A boss's main objective is to ensure that his progress does not stop, and it might involve your career growth or not. He may even ask you to do random things if it benefits him/her. Thus, while dealing with a boss, you have to work hard and smart. Still, you also have to worry about the soft parameters, such as highlighting your achievements to other stakeholders by not making your boss upset or putting your point in a meeting without sidelining your boss or promoting your brand without making your boss your rival. Because in any case, your promotion and increment, no matter what, will be decided by your boss only.

Having a good reporting manager is mostly luck, but if you do not get one, then definitely you should persist to ensure your career growth within the organisation. Never back off from such a situation because it can be and will be changed if you just persist hard enough in the right direction.

So, now it becomes essential to identify the right direction or in difficult situations, what will be the right course of action? In such cases, everyone needs a mentor who can guide you in such a situation. A mentor's job is not to help you within the organisation by pulling some strings, but his job is to give you the right direction to focus. Also, his job is to keep you in the right direction so that you do not lose focus. In any case, the work needs to be done by you only, which will make you more experienced. Thus, a mentor can be any person within the organisation or outside the organisation. He might be from the same field or have extensive work experience but from an altogether different domain. But you know what, it does not matter because a mentor helps you in all your soft goals, and he/she will support you to gain clarity on your actual goals.

Every successful person has some or another person as a mentor. Just read any biography, you will find that the famous personalities had mentors to guide them to achieve success in their career. It didn't matter whether that person was an expert in that respective field or not. But the crucial thing about having a mentor is that you get a second opinion on which path to proceed from the available options. I know it is difficult to find a perfect mentor who can listen to your problems and can assist you in making the correct choice. Here's a proposition from my end, if I can be of any help in this regard, then you can connect with me on the mail ID manishdatta.rajul@gmail.com. My purpose with this book was to guide the young professionals, and if being a mentor can give you a push in the right direction, then definitely yes, I will do it; why not?

As in this section, we are focusing on how to build a good relationship with a manager. So it is important to note that multiple factors might look trivial in your daily work habits but are extremely crucial to build a healthy relationship with your boss. These factors might be the way you provide updates over a mail or the way you share credit for a job well done with your boss, or it might be as trivial as the way you address him in the morning. In the long run, such factors play a vital role in your career growth within the company.

Let's discuss the most crucial communication tool you will use in your corporate job day-in and day-out, Mails. You might be using Outlook, Thunderbird or a simple Gmail. But no matter what system you use, you must know all the basic skills that can aid your productivity.

Whether you are working from an office or home or from an off-site location, being proficient in communicating through emails will ensure that you provide updates to your bosses and relevant stakeholders on time and with clear phrases.

It will not be wrong to invest some time to improve your typing skills. To have 90 words per minute (wpm) is godlike, but anything over 50 wpm will be good enough to get your daily tasks to be complete on time. You can check your typing speed on 10fastfingers.com or any such website. You can also let me know yours by filling the google form link:

https://forms.gle/Lt8eFcFpGZMNDvG79

By being proficient with the Email ecosystem and with good typing speed, it becomes easier to have a proper reporting mechanism with your manager for all the tasks you are handling. For example, during the Covid-19 pandemic, the work from home culture started, so it became even more important that your managers know how much time you are investing in the work and how hard you are working to have zero escalations from other stakeholders. Thus, I use to send a weekly task tracker in a very crisp and simple format, highlighting the tasks that I have finished, the update on the ongoing tasks with timeline, and the new tasks assigned to me. This way, my manager is updated and will know how much loaded I am. The task tracker also helps him if the skip level manager asks for any update on any assigned task from him. So in such cases, he never has to disturb me and can directly share the update alone.

This brings us to the next important point: who should get the credit for a job well done. Usually, people are always confused about whether their manager should take the credit or not. If you are doing the end-to-end closure of a job, then does your manager gets any recognition or not. In ninety per cent of cases, it happens that your managers will try to pitch in when the job gets done so that he earns some points as well. Now you will bypass your manager when a task gets completed and report the same directly to the skip level manager. So that it gets highlighted in the organisation that you are single-handedly responsible for this job, but do remember that this will affect your relationship with your reporting manager, and this will not do any good to you in the future. Because always remember your career growth still depends a lot on your manager only. Unless and until you interact with your skip level managers regularly, then only it is beneficial that you start giving updates on tasks directly. Otherwise, this is only going to harm you. Because after showcasing one job, then you are back to working with your manager only. But this time, it will be different because this time, instead of just taking credit, you have created an impression that you are working alone, so your reporting manager will ensure that none of your jobs gets completed smoothly. Many a time, your manager will impose redundant work activities which will make your job even harder. Your manager even starts speaking badly about you in front of top leadership. Remember, the other way around is impossible because you are not interacting with the top leadership as frequently as your manager does.

Thus, always remember that your manager might take credit for your job. This is where you get to learn the difference between a boss and a leader. A leader will put you forward to take the credit because, in his corporate career lifespan, a leader already has taken praises so many times for his own tasks, so now he does not need to steal credit from others. But a boss is just working to bring himself in the limelight, no matter what, which means he might jeopardise your career. So always ensure to tread lightly with your manager and guarantee a good working relationship with your manager. This will help you out definitely in the future because credit is not the only thing that you share with your manager. Sometimes escalations might come for a delayed task, and that's when a healthy relationship with your manager helps.

Handling the escalations in the corporate environment is not just something you learn and do it. I believe it's more about the experience in the corporate environment. It's an Art. Because the correct way to handle an escalation depends on multiple external factors like your manager, the team from which it is coming, the severity of escalation, how important it is for all the teams, and whether that escalation was actually for you or is it just randomly pin-pointing you? All these parameters make handling the escalation even more complex, and each escalation might require its own approach.

But one thing that can always save you from making that escalation does not affect your career progression is to be clear about the issue for which escalation was raised. No one wants to deal with an employee who has no clarity of what portfolio is he handling. Always have the important numbers on your tip and be aware of all the things happening in your work domain. This includes internally in your organization as well as externally in the industry.

If an escalation comes in any case, whether it is your fault or not, try to always focus on the solution. Period. In a room full of people, everyone will listen and appreciate the employee talking about the solution and not justifying his mistake. This is even more true when the money is at stake. Once the problem is resolved, then you can try to defend yourself. But at that escalated moment, everyone will be interested in solving the problem, and you should align your priorities accordingly only.

In any organization, you will always find few people who will no matter what, but they just know the way of escalation only to get things done. Even though in the first place, things have been delayed by them only, but now they will be escalating the matter to the topmost level in your category to get the issue resolved when it is pending in your bucket. A very effective way that I usually use in my work environment to deal with such employees is to befriend them. This way, people will usually call you up to let you know the actual urgency of the matter without escalating. They will plead their case, and it also makes you understand the real urgency related to the end-user. This way, the task gets completed without involving any senior management employee. In any case, you would be the one who you would be finishing the job, whether the other guy escalated the matter or not. So the approach of making friends helps everyone out and creates a win-win situation for all.

But if an escalation was raised, then the first thing you must focus on solving the issue at hand. Once the issue is resolved, be sure to report the same to all the relevant stakeholders. This helps to bring down the fire and to showcase how urgently it has been taken up. If possible, do highlight the real reason for the escalation. Do not pinpoint a single person, but identify the fault in the process and which must be rectified. This is the correct way to avoid the same mistakes to save your time and the company's resources in the future by preventing repetitive mistakes. Once the issue has been resolved, the reporting process may seem futile to you, but it is the most important one, and if you are not doing the reporting part now, you will definitely understand the same in the future.

Great managers are born by how well they handle such critical situations. Because at the time of ratings and yearly appraisal, these things will affect you a lot, and, in that case, you surely want people to remember the way you handle the escalation, not the escalation itself.

Ratings and incentives calculations are nowhere perfect in any of the organization. Some might like the situations, and some might not. And this is perfectly fine because it depends a lot on your profile, your manager, your skip-level manager and the organization's goals. Thus, it sometimes might become challenging to showcase your hard work if things are not aligned in your favour. In the current scenario, it is also that all companies will have the ratings part matching to your results and not the hard work you put in. And that's perfectly fair. Everyone is in the corporate environment if focused on earning the best they can and not favouring others.

If things are going well in the organization and you are satisfied with the rating structure, then there's nothing to worry about the process. If you want, you can skip the following few pages and directly move to the next chapter. But if things are not going well and you are struggling to achieve a good rating in the organization no matter what you do. Then the subsequent pages are the most important in this book for you.

The most effective method that I find helpful in getting good appraisal ratings is the Ask it → Do it → Earn it approach. People often struggle with a good rating because they might be putting so many efforts into completing the tasks, but these tasks were nowhere aligned to your KRAs, your team's KRAs, and your function's KRAs. It might even happen that you might be just putting so much effort to help another guy in another department achieve his/her KRAs. Nothing's wrong with helping out other people but do so once you have settled your own boat. Even in flights, it is advised to put on an oxygen mask first on yourself then help others. Similarly, in a corporate environment, everyone is on their own.

A person has been appointed for a job as per his/her capabilities: nothing more or nothing else. So first, focus on your own goals and targets, then you can definitely go out and help others. If still time permits, then definitely ask your team to give you more responsibilities to handle.

My thought is that, in any case, you would be at least spending nine hours a day, five days a week in the office. If you are giving this much time in the office, you might as well utilize this whole time to do something productive that gives you recognition within the organization. This thought process is aligned to the Ask it → Do it → Earn it approach.

At first, you ask what is required from your end to get a good rating. The next step is to just focus on completing the same and do not leave any stone unturned. With this approach, nothing can stop the last (Earn it) step from happening. If you have delivered whatever was expected from your end, then you definitely deserve a good rating, and, in such a case, your manager can't give any excuse for not giving a good rating. If the manager does so, then it's time to hunt for a better team. And I meant to hunt, not search, which means do it whatever it takes and does not rely on external factors to bring opportunities to you. It is your career progression that is at stake, and it demands a hundred percent from you.

Remember, you are in charge, and no one else is. When I started my corporate career, I wasn't so sure how to handle the appraisal season. I thought I'll automatically get what I deserve. But that's not the case. At first, I didn't focus much on what needs to be done from my end. But when I started applying this approach, then next year onwards in every review meeting, my only question to my manager was 'How do I get one rating?' (One being the best rating and five being the worst rating. It might be different as per the organization, but you get the gist.) That's it—nothing more and nothing less.

One last key factor that helps in getting a good rating is by having a good working relationship with all relevant key stakeholders. These good working relationships definitely help in a long way, and we would discuss the details in the next chapter.

# Building Relationships

In a corporate environment, your job usually will not be like a lone warrior type. You will be required to interact with multiple users and colleagues regularly to deliver a required task on time. These interactions are necessary because responsibilities are divided within a single team between multiple employees to deliver the best result for the company.

So you might handle a sourcing/procurement portfolio, and your teammate will be looking after the material management part. So, to buy a specific requirement, you might close the best rates, but without the support from the material management team, you will not be able to inward the requirement into your warehouse. Similarly, when the invoice processing part comes in at that time, you will have to connect with the billing team to process the invoices on time.

Now, you might be thinking, why building a good relationship is essential in such cases? Everyone has their defined jobs, and in the current working scenario, TATs are also assigned for each job so that things will happen on their own? You are partly correct and partly not.

Things will happen on their own unless and until some hiccups come into the process. Everything is aligned as per the requirement, and all the data is provided, then you will not have to worry about anything. But whenever there is a diversion from the standard defined process, at that moment, things become complicated. A good relationship will help you a long way because every problem has a solution, actually more than one solution. So, when a problem arises, a person might tell you the standard solution, which might be cumbersome. But due to his experience in that specific domain, he will be knowing another easy way as well to resolve the same problem, and that's when the relationship becomes paramount. This small thing may sometimes help you out in a big way.

Make a note that having a good relationship with everybody is a vital resource and never take this precious resource lightly. Take favours from other people, only when it is desperately needed. Because it is a give and take model, and you can't ask people always to help you out, just because you sugarcoated everything you say and behaved nicely all the time. They might come for help when they needed it, and there is nothing wrong with helping out, but helping them out may be difficult if their ask is not under your control.

People might ask for a favour where it is required to do some extra-legal work or against your morale, but now you can't refuse because that same person had showered multiple favours in the past when you had asked them to help you out without even thinking about the consequences. So try to focus and do your job by yourself only, and if you can do nothing else, then only take favours from others.

A much better way to work on this is by being the first guy to help others. Every time someone asks you to help out, make an extra effort to help your colleagues, team members, and other employees. This is the best way to earn respect and be in the good books of others. This way, you can rely on them in the future to help you out when the need arises. Especially with your colleagues, with whom you will be working the maximum number of hours, and without their support, the job will become harder for you. Thus, I can not stress enough how important it is to build a good working relationship within the corporate environment with your colleagues and team members.

Time will also come when you are not able to provide support due to time constraint or resource crunch. In such situations, the ability to say NO is also needed. With the current workload on the employees, everyone is just overstretched with multiple responsibilities. So you might be very busy with your tasks, and you are just not able to spare a single minute for any extra work. It is always better to refuse to help in such cases because remember, as discussed in the previous chapter, help yourself first, then focus on others. But remember to be polite while refusing to help. Just calmly put your points forward and explain them. Everyone understands that a single person can handle only limited things at a time. If he doesn't understand and nags you to provide help still somehow, then either he is really in a desperate situation where you are his only hope, or he is a guy with no moral values. In such cases, you should assess the situation and take a call accordingly because if someone cannot understand your genuine concerns for not helping out, then you shouldn't waste your valuable time on him.

This is a give and take relationship. You help out so that when the need arises, the people are ready to support you. That's just purely business. But in the corporate place, you will encounter people who will selfishly ask for help every time but will never respond when you need some help. They will just smile and will carry on with their business without remorse or regret. The best tip to handle such people is just to stay away from them and maintain distance from them as far as you can. If everything for them is business, then surely the same needs to be reciprocated from your end as well. You have to focus on the job at hand and must not waste even a single second on them.

If you have little money and have multiple options to invest, would you want to invest that money on a low returning asset or, even worse, on a negative returning asset? Ask yourself. Surely now, you would always want to maximize your returns. Similarly, time is money, and you cannot afford to lose your precious time on non-value adding things. You have to treat time as your most valuable resource. Just count the value of your time (by dividing your annual salary into 365 days). Now think, do you want to waste even a single day in any wasteful activities? This helps in making you more efficient and in prioritizing things that can provide better results in your life.

When I watched The Dark Knight movie from the Batman saga, the single most important dialogue that I liked, which is still stuck with me, is "If you are good at something, then don't do it for free" – Joker. You cannot underestimate this dialogue enough. I believe most successful people knowingly or unknowingly follow this principle to get the best output from their time. If it is just a waste of time if you are providing services for free in which we are good at it. Then definitely, we shouldn't even think about doing things where there is no return; even worse is doing something which brings negative result in the long run.

If you ensure that you are getting paid for what you are worth, then people who are employing you or taking help from you will know what you are worth and will surely respect you as well. Doing things for free makes the talent lose its worth. Because everyone knows that nothing good comes for free, everything has its price. Here, my point is not that you should always charge for your work. But my point is that other employees should respect the hard work you put within the organization, which will not happen overnight. You will have to make a dedicated effort for multiple tasks assigned to you. Your colleagues from different teams will respect you if you get the assignments completed on time within the defined TAT and sometimes even before that for urgent cases. Your team will respect you if you are always there to guide them on the process or provide a second opinion and support them in brainstorming new ideas. Your manager will appreciate your work if you are working without any escalations and doing the best you could.

All these extra effort activities help you earn respect and be in other people's good books. Being in good books helps you in the long term at the time of appraisal and promotion. But remember the important mantra, help yourself before lending out your hand to others.

Being in the good books of your team members helps at the time of internal reviews as well. Your manager may not comment good about you, but the rest of the team members will support you. They will highlight your good work, and then your manager has to go along with the team to be in your favour. Good work has never harmed anyone.

But many times, with so much work you are doing, you might tend to be arrogant instead of being polite. This simple change in your behaviour will start ruining all your excellent work. Instead of appreciating you for putting extra effort whenever you are helping them, they will begin to take help from you but will talk about your arrogance. This does not help anybody, and this will tarnish your image within the organization. You have to remember that these are your colleagues and not your close friends. You are working in a corporate environment where everything is judged and noticed. Even if you are going through some personal problems, no one will be bothered to care about it unless and until it affects them. So treat your team members like your colleagues only, and do not let your behaviour affect your performance in the office.

Sometimes, while getting too familiar within the office with everyone, you might start taking things lightly, and you might begin to say whatever comes to your mind. This usually does not work negatively with team members, but it indeed affects your relationship with your boss, where it matters the most. I typically try to avoid such situations where I blabber about anything by using ‘SIR’ annotation to my boss and super boss and so forth. As I tend to create good bonds with all the team members, annotating SIR to my boss helps me create a specific boundary between us. I would never cross that boundary which could affect our professional working environment. Because whatever happens, when the problems arise, my boss will be the first person who will enter into the picture. Whether he helps in a problematic situation or not, he mustn't make it worse just to fulfil a personal vendetta.

## Facing a Problem

If you are working in a high-pressure environment, which almost all corporate offices have, then no matter how smart or organized you are, you will face a challenge in the task assigned to you one day or another.

Sometimes you face a challenge when your profile changes and you didn't get a proper knowledge transfer from the previous employee. Sometimes, you get additional responsibilities over and above what you are already handling, increasing the workload and making it difficult to follow up on everything. Sometimes the users are not supportive, while sometimes, the system doesn't respond as per your wishes.

Thus, in short, the changes bring uncertainty in the working environment, which leads to problematic situations where you cannot meet the deadlines or satisfactory work requirements. But you know what, in life, change is the only constant. So, no matter how hard you try to avoid problems, but in any case, they will find a way in your corporate life, unless and until you do not try something new. But monotonous life will bring down the satisfaction level, which we have already discussed in the previous chapters.

So that only working solution remains is to resolve such problem and bring balance to your working environment. In such cases, almost all the time, you only have to work and identify the solution. Also, please note that sometimes you will have to think outside the box to arrive at a better solution that works with your working style.

While finding a new solution or implementing an existing one, one thing that supports you is having a good manager. A manager who understands your working style and appreciates the level of efforts you are putting in to get the job done will make your job easier and worthy. It also happens that this might be the first time you are handling such a job, but your manager, who has a long working experience in the same domain, will provide some pointers that can help you tackle the fundamental problems. Your manager's experience also allows you to steer the task at hand in the right direction from day one. Thus, it becomes more and more important to have a good manager who can support your career growth and make the job easier by not reducing the workload but by giving a proper direction.

No matter what happens, who's your manager or what's the task given to you? All these are external factors. In the end, finding the solution for the problem will depend only on the approach you adopt. As you start completing more and more tasks in your profile, the more experience you gain, the better your approach will become day-by-day. To fast track this process into getting better results from day one, your manager can act as a catalyst to give you a head start.

Also, to gain experience, you must explore the problem and try to find multiple options for the solution by yourself at first. The more you explore, the better you will become in that job. As I have mentioned previously, Thomas Edison didn't just know how to make a bulb, but he also did know more than two thousand ways from which you cannot make an operating bulb. Thus, experience matters.

Experience is not about what you have done in the past but about your ability to do things in the future. It is about your capability to tackle the problems that lie ahead by learning from your past mistakes.

Always have a solution-based approach instead of having a more generalized problem-based approach. I have seen that most of the new entrants will bother their manager when they face a problem. They will not put a single second into first exploring that problem by themselves. Thus, they just keep progressing in solving a single set of problems they face by their manager's solution. They miss out on all those learnings that they would have gained if they approached to find the solution for a problem by themselves. They would have known at least three more options and why they would not work. It might even be possible that having a quest to find a solution by yourself, you might end up on a better solution than what your manager would have given.

Also, with a solution-based approach, even your manager will appreciate that you worked out yourself. Instead of going to your superiors with a problem, go to them with at least three solution options and ask them to guide you in identifying the better one. This method is just to get their go-ahead. Now, suddenly think about the approach. With the solution-based approach, the solution is entirely yours, and your superiors just helped you pick the better one and provide the confirmation. It might happen that if you have gone to your manager before finding the solution, then he might have suggested the same solution in an instant, but with the solution-based approach, the solution is yours, and the credit for solving the problem goes to you. You are now not just the doer, but you are slowly and gradually moving towards a path of becoming a leader with experiences.

When you are handling a vast portfolio, then it will happen that you will be stuck with no clue on how to proceed forward. Or it will be that case, where you have proceeded with a solution, but it backfired. In such cases, an experience of a leader will help you to move out of the problem. But it still matters how you present the situation to your leaders. Whether you ask them to focus on the issue at hand or ask them to focus on you who could not solve the problem?

One crucial skill that I learned in a management school is presenting and putting across your point. Actually, it was less I studied in school and more about how I learned this through multiple experiences during my corporate career. When you are facing a problem, and there is no other option but to ask your superiors to pitch in and provide help, then in such cases, collect as much data about the problem as possible. You should not leave any stone unturned. This will help you to answer all the questions that will be asked by your superiors when you address the problem with them.

There are few important things that you should cover while explaining a problem, like

- Justify: Give a clear and crisp justification for the reason behind the problem. You should try to provide details so that everyone's focus is on the problem at that moment because finding a solution is more important, rather than identifying who's fault it is and play a blame game.
- Put in your best foot: Try to be on your best behaviour. Deliver the updates in the best possible way so that chances of it backfiring on you gets minimal. Be prepared with the data so that you can answer all the questions without even looking into your laptop.
- No Mistakes: There should not be any possibilities of making a mistake in the calculations and the numbers related to the problem. There should not be any margin of error in it. Because you are already treading on edge thus, you can leave nothing on chances. Check, then double-check, and be assured that everything is correct. Then again, check once

more. You can't stress how important this is. Because sometimes, mistakes pass by that we didn't even really thought were there in a high-pressure environment, and such an environment will always be there when a problem arises and is escalated to the top management.

- Complete Picture: When people are under high stress, they miss out on minor details. Even when they explain, they tend just to skip out some details to make the discussion less complicated. But believe me, without the complete information, people may understand the problem, but they will miss out on the background and the real cause for it. This might lead to a longer time in finding a solution, or if some information comes into highlight afterwards, it might look even worse than before. So it is always better to give all the information in one go, without any filtering and in a clear-crisp manner. I always try to do this in a storyline way, where I take the management through the events in the sequence of their occurring with minor changes.
- Dilemma: Taking help from the superiors is one way of approaching the problem when it is getting out of your hand. But you can also ask your teammates to pitch in if you think they can have a better solution. Some of your teammates will be working in the team long before you came into the organization; thus, they might better understand the organization. Sometimes, it happened to me that the problem that

I was thinking is just way too big, but some of my teammates had faced a similar problem in the past, and they just made a call and resolved it in an instant. So it never harms anyone in asking for help.

No matter what the problem, it is always better to give your team leaders the information about the problem rather than coming from someone else as an escalation. Thus, always be a step ahead of other stakeholders, and just take a call if you think that it is time that your leaders should pitch in. This will also help in making good bonding with your superiors, with a caveat that if they can solve the problems. You ask for help, and if they can provide support on this, then this showcases that they are better experienced than you, and it creates a mentor-mentee bond between you and your leader.

Many people miss out on having a good relationship with a leader because they do not focus on important points. This is not their fault, and they are not doing this purposefully. But this usually happens because people do not know what it likes and takes to be a leader.

# Being a Leader

The way the old saying goes that the grass is greener on the other side of the road, the same way, we do not know the hardship the leader has to go through unless and until we get to that position. As a leader, multiple factors play a role in making a decision. Sometimes a decision looks so simple to us, and we think, why can't a leader take such a simple call? But in reality, we do not know the complete background behind and what is at stake in that decision.

When you climb the corporate ladder and get to a level where you have multiple members in your team, in such a situation, the job becomes more about the way you handle your team members and less about you doing as part of the actual groundwork. Your job is to ensure that your team is working at its full potential to get the job in hand finished with spectacular results. This sounds simple, but in reality, it becomes harder and harder. Because it is easier to do a job by yourself than getting someone else to do the same for you. But in any case, you, as a single person, can do one task spectacularly but cannot perform multiple tasks at once. Thus, the team is provided to do the ground job for you, and you lead them to deliver the same spectacular results with your guidance.

First things first, you should not fall into the trap of following your manager literally. Do not follow the things that your manager does wrong. Everyone has his/her style of working. So you can have yours. Learn from other managers, pursue the things they do correctly and do not follow the things they do incorrectly. Find a better way, and implement that into your style of working. Every day is a testing ground, and only by testing out some new possibilities, you will be able to bring something new into the working culture that suits your team members.

Even when people get promoted and start handling a team, they just focus on their performance only, even though it requires your team to work at odd hours to deliver a key initiative, then so be it. But it is crucial to notice that you are responsible for your team's well-being and working culture as a leader. Otherwise, you will become a typical corporate boss about whom everyone cribs in their social group. So, take responsibility and see what requires to make the environment more workable.

The team's efficiency also depends on how you allocate the task. In a factory, the ground workers perform the same set of job in the entire shift so that the learning curve can be achieved faster and output can be increased significantly. Similarly, you can assign tasks within your team so that everyone is responsible for a small set of tasks and can master these tasks in a short period. This method helps achieve the results faster and is better than giving the complete end-to-end responsibility to a single person. This method also helps to make the ground force comfortable in a job. The more comfortable they are, the lesser the chances of them switching a job. At a lower level, the attrition rate is anyways higher, so focus on making the ground force stronger and try to retain them. But do note that this method should be applied basis on the type of profile you are handling. Like in a sales profile, usually complete responsibility for deal closure lies with the sales team. They will take help from internal stakeholders, but only a single Spoc is assigned to the customer so that the customer gets a better service experience.

Allocating tasks to your team is also a skill, and you should take this responsibility seriously. While assigning tasks to your team, kindly think through them clearly and plan how to deliver the required results. Remember that you are a thinking machine, while your team will provide support to deliver the task by working on the ground level. So the more you assign the tasks in a planned and clear manner, the better results you will get from your team. When your manager assigns you a task without any clear guidelines, think how frustrating you find that job. Thus, we have to avoid all such mistakes and ensure that we provide tasks to our team members with clear guidelines. From my experience, having so much work is not a problem usually, but having work but not knowing how to finish it – is the actual problem.

If I give you a job to create a space shuttle without any explicit instructions or a team, then definitely it's an impossible job. But for the same job, if a team is assigned to you who has experience in it and you are given a job according to your knowledge to govern a team and ensure that the space shuttle gets built within a timeline, then this definitely makes the job doable.

Assign clearly planned tasks to your team, and you would be surprised by the efficient results they deliver to you.

You have made a clear plan and assigned the tasks to your team so that they can deliver properly. But still, every time, your team cannot deliver an assigned task within the timeline. You might have given them a month for a job that should have taken them two weeks max, but still, they cannot deliver the same. In such cases, the two factors play an essential role. One we have already discussed in the previous chapters, i.e. Parkinson's law. The more time available, the more the job going to be stretched. The second factor for the delay is procrastination. It is ingrained in all human beings that if more time is available, then things will generally take a back step.

The key here is to create a plan for delivering tasks along with timelines. Create checkpoints to measure that if the team is going at the pace required or is lagging. Also, always provide time that is actually needed to deliver a job, no more, no less. Neither you should create an environment of procrastination, nor you should make an unnecessary urgency. These things affect the quality of results. With clear and defined checkpoints, you would never be tensed about delivering the job on time if everything is going as per the plan. This helps your subordinates as well. You might be well versed in delivering a big assignment, but that might not be true for your team. The big job assigned might be their first job with such deliverables. In such cases, no matter how much time you provide, it is always not going to be enough, and the team will always be tensed, no matter how good they are performing. Thus, checkpoints with delivery timelines provide them feedback, whether they should buckle up or keep working on this pace only.

Building a team and making them efficient are only two parts of having a good team. Every leader has to go through this process. But the last and the most crucial part is to retain your team of good people. You have put your blood and sweat into finding good peoples and training them to deliver the results every single time within the timelines. So undoubtedly, you do not want to lose such people to other teams.

Employees start looking for another job if the management does not acknowledge their hard work. Also, if their requests are being ignored, this also triggers them to look for an outside job offer. The request may be that they need a promotion or a raise for the work they are doing, which they deserve. Sometimes, a leader forgets to focus on their team member, and he can e correct that quickly because it is a job that needs to be done by you only. But this becomes harder when you cannot support your team as a leader because the management's goals are aligned differently. In such cases, you have to fight for your team. If your team has worked hard enough to provide support to you to achieve your

KRAs, then surely now it's your time to fight for them to get the things they deserve. This small act of standing for your team differentiates a leader and a typical corporate boss.

As a leader, it is also vital to ensure that job delivered is up to the mark. It should at least meet the level of performance that you would deliver. Do not tolerate sub-standard work. No matter how good your relationship is with your team. Everyone is here to do their job first, and then the rest of the things matter. Never cheat with your career, and your team should follow the same as well. Be rigid to the level of performance you require from your team, but yet be flexible enough to provide support as and when your teams require it from you to deliver the task at hand.

The learning from mistake piece that we discussed at the start of this book also applies here. But here, you would not be the one who will be making those mistakes, but you will be the one who needs to recognize the difference between praiseworthy and blameworthy mistakes.

To make your team grow to its full potential, you must build a learning culture and, at all times, should avoid the blame game.

The leader must define the level of mistakes that we could make depending on the industry we are in and the kind of job we are handling. If you are in the R&D division, then you are in the discovery business and making mistakes is part of the job. In this role, you would not be able to deliver the best result without making a mistake. The faster we fail, the faster we learn to bring success. Thus, mistakes are good in this role.

But the same ideology of making mistakes will not hold true if you are in a manufacturing business. Here, everything is tried and tested, and you just have to ensure that processes are running as per the defined guidelines. Making mistakes will harm the customer satisfaction level and may instil penalties on delivering defective products. Thus, this will lead to significant losses for the company.

As a leader, your job is to bring the correct practice of learning from failures but even more important is to understand when to declare defeat, especially when an experimental course is followed. These decisions are made based on the experiences that you will gain by making many mistakes by yourself as a leader.

Following all these mantras, laws and rules, will help you to become a better leader to gain prosperity in your career life. But finally, it boils down to only one thing, and that is being peaceful. We have discussed all these things in the previous chapters are to ensure that we have a peaceful and satisfying work life. Life is too short to make it hell at the workplace where you would be spending one-third of your life. Everyone gets only one life; thus, it is important to make it enjoyable and worth living. In the following few chapters, we will discuss how to be peaceful and what changes we can bring to make our corporate life filled with satisfaction.

# Work-Life Balance

People started going for a corporate job to earn more money and to have a secured future. The corporate jobs provided them comfort, knowing that no matter what happens, there will be enough food on their plates the next day, the next month, the next year and so on. Because suddenly, they are not dependent on the seasonal factors, like people in the agriculture sector.

But as things progressed, people got too focused on this corporate job and were sucked into this web, and they forgot how to live in a true sense. The true purpose was never to make bad choices and have a miserable life. If you are earning way more than what is required, but still you are not at peace in your mind, then there is something wrong with how you live your life. You have to address that immediately because we cannot underestimate the importance of mental health.

Many times, people get too focus on their job that they forget about their personal life. It's mainly because, in the early stages of your career, people prioritize corporate life over personal life, hoping that if we achieve big at the start of the career, then we can settle down in later stages or take early retirement at the age of 40. They prioritize all fun activities for the after-40 stage of life.

People forget that no one can predict that what will happen after 15-20 years from now. But most importantly, who made this rule that you can enjoy after-40 only? Who defined that you can focus on one single thing in your life at once? Living a happy and peaceful life is just about finding the balance. Your target in life should be to pursue the right balance between all things that matter in your life at a given point in time.

I am a big fan of Japanese culture because it is all about finding the right balance in your life, whether it is related to work or studies or love life. The culture focuses on achieving the right balance between all of them. Actually, it focuses on finding the balance that suits you, which will bring you and your mind at peace.

The same knowledge about achieving a balance we should apply in our daily life as well. It is not fair to our body and mind that we rigorously burn them out in hopes that we will focus on the enjoyment in the later stages of life once we are well settled. Because it does not bring you any comfort, instead it pushes you to have an exhaustive work life.

With no pleasure in the daily activities, you will start hating your corporate life as well. Thus, it is important to bring balance. Whenever I used to sit for studies, my mother had this practice to reward me at every small interval during the study. The checkpoints were fixed accordingly only. She used to keep a small piece of chocolate at the end of every paragraph so that once I finish that paragraph, I can have my reward. Eventually, it started happening that while reading, I would get hooked to the book's story, and then my focus shifted from the chocolate at the end of the paragraph to what's going to happen in the following line. I guess the act of these small rewards helped me to create a habit of reading regularly.

The same thing needs to be applied in our life as an adult as well. This time instead of paragraphs, we can reward ourselves with checkpoints in work life. You can change the reward from chocolate to something bigger and more adventurous like a trip to a nearby secluded mountain or an afternoon at the beach or sunset at a hill station or any fun activity with your friends - painting, music, reading, etc. These things will ensure that your life does not become boring and is continuously filled with happy moments. This will, in turn, make you more comfortable and at ease in the corporate environment. You will be more focused on performing your office tasks because you reward yourself at regular intervals of time for doing a job well done.

But still, while doing all these activities at once, you will be losing out on something or another. People will suggest to you that there is no gain without pain, and that's partly true. But what's even more important is to focus on what pain are you ready to take. For example, if you are sacrificing a promotion to have a week-long trip on a beach. But while sitting at a beach, if you are still cribbing about not getting a promotion, then it's not worth it. This happened because you didn't think about if you are ready to take the pain of not getting a promotion. If you had prioritized the things at first, then you will surely avoid the trip.

But in the other case, if you have foregone a promotion so that you get more time to spend with your newborn baby, then the same thing of not getting a promotion might not bother you. Because the act of spending more time with family is now on a higher priority for you than spending a single second more at the job. In this scenario, before making a decision, you simply prioritized what is more important.

| | | | | |
|---|---|---|---|---|
| Spending time with a newborn baby | > | Getting a Promotion | > | Spending time at the beach |

So always prioritize and then decide what you are ready to sacrifice to have a better and peaceful life.

Always follow the things that motivate you to live a better life day by day. Continuous improvements can only guarantee a better life.

Even in the corporate environment, do not chase what others are doing. Everyone has different goals and different priorities. Suppose someone in the company is switching the company because of better pay, but your target is to lead a bigger team, and you think that your current organization will be able to provide you with the same. In that case, there is no point in focusing on switching the company. Just focus on your long-term goals and persist in achieving them. Nothing else matters. All these external factors will fade away against your hardship.

Remember when we talked about pain-gain and what pain are you ready to take? The same formula applies here as well. Your company will be able to provide a better working environment and a better team to lead, while the other company is providing a better pay scale. So to achieve one thing, you have to sacrifice the other. So pain-gain relationship is working here as well. But the question, out of these two, is which pain are you ready to take in order to achieve the other one? As I have explained in the previous paragraphs, you have to prioritize, and then you have to decide which pain you have to take and still be peaceful with it.

At the start of their career, people compare their success with money, but eventually, they realize that there are many other factors to assess the quality of a corporate job. According to my experience, the three main important factors that we have to look out for in a corporate job are Salary, Job Profile and Your Team, which includes your colleagues, manager, etc.

Your ideal job would be the one which provides all three of them as per your requirement. Note that here I have mentioned that it is as per your requirement and not with any specifics or standards defined in a rule book. Each individuals' requirements may differ. One person might want a manager to not interfere in their regular workings and take an update weekly only. In contrast, another person might want to work on a regular basis with their manager. So, it depends on the individual person's requirement.

In most of the scenarios, especially at the start of the career, people put too much emphasis on only one parameter of these two. That single most important parameter is salary, where you get what you expect as per the level of hard work you are putting in at the corporate job. People do not focus much on the job profile, including your location, the level of work you do, and the deliverables required from you. Are they making you grow as a professional or not? That's perfectly fine because you have a Wishlist to fulfil at the start of your career. Also, many people have education loans to pay off before they focus on other things.

People do not worry about the team as well. People usually think that this is purely on luck, of what kind of team we are getting. You might be satisfied with whatever the team is unless and until you are getting paid a hefty amount as a pay package.

But as you grow in your career and get more experienced, you will undoubtedly focus on all the parameters. If you are already at that stage, where you have an experience of at least four to five years, then you should focus on other parameters too. Because salary increase will happen on its own up to a certain level only, then it will start flattening out as you grow to a senior leadership position. At the start of your career, you might be getting a fifteen to twenty percent growth in the salary every year. But afterwards, the growth may not be more than five percent yearly. So, other parameters start playing a significant role in your decision making.

By the time you get promotions and become a senior executive, you might have exhausted your wishlist as well, so it becomes beneficial to focus on other parameters that can bring peace to your corporate life. First, identify the amount of salary that suits your requirement basis on your job location, liabilities (loans, dependents, etc.) and future personal goals. If you are already receiving that much salary, then anything more will not make much difference, and living standards won't be increasing much. But instead, to get even more compensation, you might be putting extra hours in the office, making your life miserable.

So identify what is the ideal salary at your age and as per your lifestyle, and target that much only. You should devote the rest of the focus to improving your job profile and getting a team that helps you grow. You can even spend the rest of the time generating a second income or increasing your learning level.

Indirectly, the rest of the two factors play a significant role in getting you a career that pays you even higher. Because these factors help you to build a better profile and get experienced that will have its own market value.

In the book, The Millionaire Next Door, I have read about the concept of Ideal Wealth that one should have as per his age and annual salary. The formula was given as

$$Ideal\ Wealth = \frac{\text{Annual Salary x Age in Years}}{10}$$

This is a straightforward and realistic formula that helps you to calculate whether you are on the right track or not. If not, then what amends you should make. For details about each parameter and how to optimize your wealth, I would recommend going through the book. (Details mentioned in the footnote.)

You can never be sure enough of how much money you should have. But by knowing the ideal wealth from the formula and the real wealth you have as of now, you can easily chalk out a definitive plan to reduce the difference. Once you cross that mark, where your actual wealth is more than the ideal wealth required, then you will surely attain peace from a monetary perspective. You will be assured that you are not wasting enough and you are in the right job, which is helping you to earn enough to meet your wealth goals.

One last aspect that is also important in being peaceful is personal growth. Personal growth means developing positive habits and have continuous growth in your personal life as well. This can include learning a new skill, fulfilling your wishes or just have a better family life. It can depend from person to person. But the important thing to notice is that you should not just focus on corporate life only, but rather have a balance between corporate and personal life.

Your job is just part of your life, and it is not everything. At the death bed, you should not be regretting for not doing one thing or another. People usually regret missing out on doing things that they have planned but thought they have enough time. That is the only goal that everyone should have.

Multiple factors play in work life that are out of your control sometimes, but personal growth is in your hands, and no matter how busy you are, always keep time to focus on your personal life as well.

# Office Politics

You might be wondering why I have kept a separate chapter to talk about this? In the previous chapters, I have not mentioned a single thing about office politics. The fact is whether you accept it or not, but office politics do play a significant role in everyone's career, and people do come across this on a regular basis. It is a tricky matter, and it is important to know how to deal with this. Thus, it definitely requires a particular focus and a dedicated chapter to understand it properly.

First things first, let's clarify what office politics is? It simply means that the actions you take or the behaviour you possess regarding competition for status or to achieve power at the workplace.[3]

It mainly arises when there is a difference in opinion between your co-workers or office colleagues. So, to put your point forward, you start influencing the decision-maker by using tactics that benefit your career growth. People might use it for a very trivial requirement as just getting a laugh on someone to most urgent concerns such as getting a promotion. In short, one starts relying on this for career progression instead of focusing on delivering the best possible result for the job at hand. Thus, people start opting for the shortcut method instead of achieving the results through hard work and persistence.

---

[3] https://languages.oup.com/google-dictionary-en/

Many people think that the correct way to be safe from office politics is to be a part of it and employ this yourself before anyone else can do it on you. You start keeping track of everyone else's views and moves. But you may not be any more wrong about this. An HBR article, 'Playing Office Politics Without Selling Your Soul',[4] suggests another way, but I believe it is better to focus on more productive things.

Office politics gives nothing but unnecessary tension to your head. Instead of focusing on your job and your performance level, you will be wasting your time watching out your back if you focus on playing an upper hand in office politics.

People often complain that they do not have time to complete their work or the work assigned to them is just so overwhelming and is just impossible to complete. But 9 out of 10 times, people waste their time in non-value adding activities and are decreasing their productivity day by day. So, when the appraisal time comes, employees have to resort to the shortcut and try to get good ratings by playing office politics.

---

[4] "Playing Office Politics Without Selling Your Soul" by Robert B. (Rob) Kaiser, Tomas Chamorro-Premuzic, and Derek Lusk, HBR September 2017 https://hbr.org/2017/09/playing-office-politics-without-selling-your-soul

An important point to notice here is that even if you are not getting involved in such petty office politics, but it is worthwhile to save your back when the time requires. The correct mantra is 'Never be a part of office politics, nor let anyone make you a part of it. If someone is bad-mouthing against you or is trying to hurt your work, then you should definitely save yourself. Because you being good to others does not guarantees that others will reciprocate in the same manner.

When you work together with your colleagues in the office, it is natural that you become friends and start involving them in your personal lives. But always keep a boundary between the colleagues. You never know what might be a light-hearted joke which might hurt someone so profoundly that they start ruining your career. So, have fun but keep a boundary. Being friendly is important to make good working relations with everyone, but being over-friendly might destroy all your hard work.

If you are dedicatedly working towards your tasks and not worrying about the bad people, then your colleagues, team members and superiors will appreciate your professionalism. This will help you, in the long term, to achieve larger goals because everyone knows what agenda a person is driving in the company, whether someone is working to their full potential or not.

Trust is paramount, and it takes lots of time and effort to achieve that from colleagues. But it takes a slight mistake or single lousy work to ruin everything. Thus, tread lightly and focus on your work only. When the time comes to get promoted or planning to get a job switch, nothing else will matter except your performance. You might get an early promotion in the company compared to your colleague, but the same colleague the very next day might leave the company for a better job. Because everyone has their own priority, and you might be focusing on the wrong agenda. Thus, it is better to focus on your personal growth with the sheer dedication that can benefit you in the long run.

Anyone who is working with political agenda may gain importance or favour in the company for a short duration only. Eventually, the team leader will change, or the person himself will switch a job for better perks and salary. In such cases, things will boil down to square one, and you can never be sure that the tactics you have employed as part of office politics will work the same way again with the new team. But nothing can beat the hard work and professionalism.

# Job Switch

People switch profiles within the company, or they change the company altogether because of many reasons. People often switch the job profile just by being emotional without having any proper knowledge of what lies ahead of them. Getting a job switch is not an easy decision, and it needs to complete thought through because it can uplift or ruin your future career prospects entirely. Thus, it is better to make such a decision with utmost certainty and without any doubts.

The three main reasons that should govern a job switch are the Job Profile, Salary Package and the Leadership Team. These three factors constitute everything related to a job that needs special attention.

The job profile in a new company will include the type of work, the amount of work, job location and relevance to your long-term goal. If all these factors in a job profile are aligned with your requirement, then that job profile will be suitable for you. It might happen that some factors might not be as per your desire, then it is better that you assess what pain you are ready to take? You might be prepared to compromise with the job location if the rest of the factors are good because currently, you are focusing on building your resume with a suitable type of work. But for someone else, it might be the case that the person wants to be nearer to their hometown so that he can be live with his parents to support them in their old age. In such a case, job location matters the most. Thus, priorities differ from person to person, and you should see what matters to you most and be focused on that only.

Next comes is the salary package. This includes the complete package, i.e. your CTC, additional bonus, perks, and the expenses you will incur with respect to fulfilling your duty at the job. Many times people do not consider the change in the living expenses while changing the job. The new job location can be farther from your home location; thus, you incur more transportation cost. It may also happen that the new job location is in an altogether different city where the living expenses are higher; thus, it nets off any increase in the salary. All these things may decrease the money that you save at the end of the month.

But again, it is more important what the individual person wants and does this meet his/her requirement. My point is just to highlight these things and that everyone should pay attention to this while considering the salary they will get with the job change.

Last but not the least, the third factor for the job switch is the leadership team. You might have heard that people do not change the job, but they change their boss. I believe that it is the ultimate truth, with the only change being that people do not change just the boss, but they look for a change in the leadership team. Your profile might not be as good as you want, and you might not be getting the salary package that you deserve, but if your manager and leadership team is good, then you still will be enjoying the job. If your manager ensures that your career is growing day by day, then you will eventually end up with the desired pay and profile. The reporting manager plays a significant role in governing where your career moves. Here, I haven't mentioned that the manager should work as an ideal manager. The requirement is that there should be a sync between you and your manager in the way you both handle a specific job at hand.

If you can get all three factors, i.e. Job Profile, Salary and Leadership Team, in a particular job that are as per your requirement, then leave everything and just switch to the new job. Because these three factors define what an ideal should be like for you. But what happens is that it is challenging to find all three things as per your requirement in a single job. One thing or another will work differently than what you want, and you will be struggling to identify the solution to that.

But it is easier to find at least two factors that meet your requirement and be satisfied with them. You can always strive for all three, but you get mostly two factors in your favour no matter what 9 out of 10 times. Now, with all the different strategies discussed in the previous chapters, you can employ those to make the remaining third factor in your favour.

People usually decide to switch a job basis a single bad experience they had in a day. But this is the worst way to make that decision because even if you change the job, there is still no guarantee that you will get all the required parameters in your favour. Mostly any job will have two out of three factors only as per your desire and that too not for long. Also, once you start working in the new company, then everything depends on your performance only. Thus, before deciding to make a switch from your current job, it is important to identify why you want to make a switch from your current job?

The reason behind the switch is equally important as the new job you get. If the reason behind the job switch is not fixed, then again, you might end up with another job with a different or similar problem. Because now you are just randomly trying to change your job without any direction and relying entirely on luck to get a job with a better fit than what you currently have.

Even if you had multiple job offers in hand, still do not just go and select the best offer among them. Without proper analysis, it is not possible to know that the best offer among them suits you perfectly. Thus, before making a pros-cons list for which new company you should move to, identify the real reason which made you unhappy in your previous stint. Unhappiness might not be the reason all the time, but what prompt you to start looking for a job. Once you identify this, you would find a job that can mitigate your feeling of unhappiness.

There are many minuscule factors in each job, which we overlook while making a job switch, but in the long run, all these factors amount to so much that they might lead to frustration and bad performance. Like for example, Job timing. I have seen many people who had taken a job which offered a higher salary and good working culture. But they forgot to check the job timings and whether these timings are aligned to their preferences or not. Always remember that the job is just part of your life and it is not the only thing. To be happy, you have to take care of your mental peace and fulfil all your personal life obligations as well, related to your friends and family.

Some companies have fixed daily working hours, while some do not have any such restrictions and want their employees to work flexibly. The only thing that employees should ensure is that the job gets done on time. But such companies usually allocate more tasks to each employee, which might lead to long working hours if you are not working effectively.

Thus, the number of working hours the job has also mattered. Although spending more hours at work does not mean that you are delivering more, but some companies do have this fixed working hours philosophy. In current times, it has become more and more important to factor in the amount of time you will be spending at the workplace, because time is limited with everyone and as the saying goes, Time is Money. So, while making a job switch, always check the working hours and how much time the job requires you to work in a week.

One friend of mine made a job switch as he got a 15% increment from his current pay. Although the job role at the present and new organization are more or less the same, but the number of working days in a week was different. In his previous organization, they had a culture of a five-day working week, but in his new organization, they had a six-day working week. Thus, instead of five, now he has to go to the office for six days. So, effectively if we see, time-wise, he dedicates 20% more time to the work than he used to. Now, if we compare the 15% salary hike with the 20% increase in the number of hours at work, the job switch doesn't look like a good choice. This is not just about the time you spent at work. It is also about how productively you spent it. My friend was highly effective at the workplace. He had a clear vision of the tasks at hand and how to finish them within the timeline. He also had a good experience in aligning his subordinates to the same goal of delivering better results. But in the new organization, he did not get any team, and the company only offloaded all the work to his shoulders. So, the sixth day of working added to his working schedule was to make sure that people do all their job by themselves. No guessing required that my friend, with his excellent impression in the previous organization, switched back to it within six months only.

You cannot measure a single factor all alone. If one thing increases, then the remaining factors might reciprocate accordingly only. In our case, if salary increases, then the amount of work might increase, or the quality of work-life balance might decrease. Every corporate is in the business to make money, and it is fair to do. But the thing that matters is that if the corporate has its goal aligned and is working accordingly, then you should too. You should also prioritize what matters to you the most, whether it is more time with family or more money in hand, and then decide to switch a job accordingly.

People usually forget that how much amount of work and type of work can influence your corporate life in the long term. Doing a large amount of work does not ensure that any value-addition will happen to your career progression. But the type of work you do matters the most, and you should look at it first. If you are doing monotonous work at the job, and even if it increases drastically, still no one will value the efforts you are putting in. Also, all monotonous activities can be and will be replaced by automation, so if you keep doing this type of work, then it makes your job vulnerable. As soon as the company feels that automation is the correct way forward, then they will learn from you and will replace you with machines that can perform a better and more consistent job.

If you are in the customer-facing or supplier-facing role, then it provides you a wide range of experience which also includes some soft quality parameters. A company cannot automate these qualitative parameters, and the way you handle certain strategic deals gives you an advantage over others. This is the experience that counts over the long term. Now, if the number of work hours increases in this domain, then still, it should be perfectly fine with you because you already have the edge over others, and you are not a replaceable resource for the company. In fact, you are an asset to the organization, which enables you to demand additional pay that you certainly deserve.

Now, you might have understood everything that I had mentioned in the previous paragraphs, and you might be agreeing that this is the correct way to proceed. But this is not like rocket science, which I have to make you understand. This is fundamental learning that everyone gains from experience, but still, many people do not follow these steps and fall into the trap of regular corporate life. This is because everyone follows a herd mentality.

It is no one's fault that people succumb to this trap, but this is how we are raised and taught since we are in school. We are programmed to avoid downfalls and then only focus on the upside potential. But if you see anywhere and in whatever field you look, only one philosophy holds true: the higher the risk, the higher the reward. Because you get paid for the risk you have taken. Only hard work is not much worth to anyone, because anyone can do the hard work without thinking. So many people are unemployed, and it is easier to fulfil the jobs requiring no thinking. If you think, this can be fulfilled by robots as well. Therefore, qualitative learning parameters are important for your career growth.

One last but the most important thing that I want to discuss is your true capability. The job you are interested in, the job that you can deliver with utmost perfection, the job that utilizes your experience.

People often take a job in a completely different field or to a different location, just for better pay or to show off in front of their friends. That's the biggest mistake you could make. Also, people mention things in their resume or during their interviews that are entirely not aligned to their goal or their expertise, just so that they can land that job. But this harms you and the company both. Because if you get that job, then you have to work in a profile that does not suit you. This harms the company as well because they hired you thinking that you are an expert, but now you will not be able to deliver the level of results expected from you. To avoid such instances, companies nowadays ask all candidates to go through multiple screening processes so that they can identify the person who is a perfect fit for the job.

People say that they wanted a job where they enjoy working, where it doesn't feel like a mundane job. They do not wish to have a stressful environment so that they can enjoy what they are doing. But still, many people end up at a job that is not in their domain of expertise, which creates a stressful environment for everybody. Identify a job that aligns with your current capabilities and with your future goals. Your ideal job should be the one that utilizes your existing knowledge and provides you ample opportunities to enhance the learning even further. This way, it would be a win-win situation for both parties.

After so much discussion, one thing is clear: a good profile matters a lot to be successful in the corporate career, be peaceful in life, and have a proper work-life balance. In the next chapter, we will discuss what goals we should have to make a profile good and how can we make it better?

# Career Goals

In the previous chapters, we talked a lot about a good profile. But what defines a good profile? You cannot solely represent a profile as good. You need a reference point of your target goal, or you need to compare how good you are at your job with respect to other people having the same years of experience to justify that you are good at what you do and is relevant to your companies as well. This way, it would be possible to define a good profile.

The best way to build a good profile is to steer it in the direction which matches your short-term and long-term goal. If your goals are defined, then you can easily chart an execution plan to achieve these goals and then stick to the plan to fulfil your goals. Nothing else matters!

But if your goals are not defined, you will always be confused to identify what should be your next steps. Whether to stick to this company and profile or you should explore new opportunities outside your current domains.

A few years back, I had a fortunate chance to meet a senior-most executive who was working in a sourcing portfolio in the supply chain division. He had his goals identified and charted into short-term and long-term goals. His long-term goal was to become the head of the supply chain division in a company and to fulfil that; he must gain experience in all five major supply chain domains. This will enable him to have a clear understanding of the end-to-end supply chain process. Thus, when he started looking for a new job once he gained significant experience in the sourcing division, he didn't explore the sourcing jobs which generally people would have done. Instead, he looked for material management jobs, which was his next target in covering all five domains.

As his goal was to become the head of the supply chain division whose job would be to oversee the functioning of the entire supply chain department, therefore, he was building his profile accordingly by gaining experience in all domains.

If another guy whose target is to become Chief Procurement Officer (CPO), who is well versed with all sourcing knowledge, then he will not switch for a job that is not relevant to sourcing portfolio and would want to gain sourcing experience from different industries like FMCG, Telecom, Manufacturing, etc.

The same principle applies to other jobs as well. If your long-term goal is to become a Chief Marketing Officer (CMO), then you would want to have a marketing experience of different products so that you can build synergies and leverage knowledge gained from one domain to another. But you cannot market properly if you do not know how that product gets sold in the market to the consumer? Thus, it is important to add a sales profile role at the start of your career as part of your short term goal. Now, by finalizing your short-term and long-term goals, you know what you are looking for and what kind of efforts you have to make to build a good, worthy profile to land any job in your desired field.

In short, all you require is the clarity with which you want to have your career progressed. Many a time, in the job interview, the interviewers usually ask for a five-year or a ten-year plan to the candidate. In these uncertain times, no one is sure what will happen in five or ten years. No one can even predict what the market is going to be like after two years. But the interviewers still ask you this question because their expectation is not that you predict your future but expect you to least have a decent enough plan for it. This planning helps them to identify if their goals and your goals are aligned or not. This benefits everyone in the long term. If the companies target is to hire a candidate and nurture them to take a senior position with key responsibilities within the company in the next five years, but your goal is to gain experience from multiple industries, then there is a misalignment in the goals and in the long-term, it will affect both the parties.

The goals of both parties should be aligned; then, only everyone will be happy in performing their jobs and delivering the result to their level best.

To achieve these goals, everyone has to go through the learning process to make themselves capable enough to handle more significant tasks efficiently. You must strategically take the next steps in your career path so that you achieve the best results you can for continuous career growth. By having a plan, you become comfortable and more focused on your job.

I hope this book gives you all the necessary stepping stones for living a peaceful and prosperous corporate

**Welcome to the Corporate world.**

**It sucks, but you will have a great time here!**

# Acknowledgements

*A heartful thanks to my lovely wife, Vaishali, for making this journey of writing a book as comfortable as it can get. Without her support through this time, this book would not have seen the light in the bookstores.*

*I would also like to thank all my friends and colleagues for sharing their experiences and helping me in gaining the key insights related to different profiles.*

# Author Bio

Manishdatta Rajul has completed his post-graduation from IIM Bangalore. He has corporate working experience in both private and government organizations. Manish was fortunate enough to work under the leadership of several leaders and with multiple teams on different projects. He loves to share his knowledge with young professionals to inspire them to focus on important corporate life goals. With this book, his target is to touch more lives and guide even more people towards success and prosperity.

Manish is basically from Uttar Pradesh but born and brought up in Gujarat. Currently, he resides in Gurgaon with his beautiful wife. Within his friends' circle and in office workgroups, Manish is a go-to guy for any advice. This book is his attempt in helping the vast audience of young professionals to navigate the tricky waters of corporate life.

# Thank You!

Love this book? Don't forget to leave a review!

Every review matters, and it matters a *lot!*

Head over to Amazon or Goodreads to leave an honest review for me.

Your reviews will help me improve the future versions of this book and bring improvements within myself.

I thank you endlessly.

www.ingramcontent.com/pod-product-compliance
Lightning Source LLC
LaVergne TN
LVHW100403181026
850499LV00037B/581
*9789354721427*